Better Homes and Gardens
How to sew for Children

MEREDITH PRESS

NEW YORK   DES MOINES

BETTER HOMES AND GARDENS CREATIVE SEWING LIBRARY, FIRST PRINTING

CREATIVE SEWING

Beautiful fabrics and exciting pattern styles make sewing more rewarding than ever. With today's new techniques and equipment, sewing can be fun for the beginner as well as the accomplished seamstress.

Better Homes and Gardens Creative Sewing Library presents sewing methods based on common sense—practical, professional tips that show how to give clothes for the whole family a "custom-made" look.

The Creative Sewing Library has been prepared under the guidance of Miss Lucille Rivers, one of America's eminent sewing experts. To help women learn the easy, professional methods of sewing she describes in the books, she has drawn upon her long experience in the field. Miss Rivers has directed her own custom salon in New York, and she has served as consultant to many leading clothing manufacturers.

She has created new styles for fashion shows, and has lectured on sewing in department stores in this country, Australia, and New Zealand. For many years Miss Rivers was sewing editor of NBC's popular "Home Show," and she has conducted sewing demonstrations on many other television programs. In the Creative Sewing Library, she shares her fashion knowledge and dressmaking experience with you.

Titles in the Creative Sewing Library are:
> *Professional Sewing Tips*
> *How to Sew for Children*
> *Pattern Adjustments*
> *Tailoring Suits and Coats*
> *Sewing Casual Clothes*

CONTENTS

Sewing children's clothes

A mother of two or more children is usually eager to learn all the short-cut sewing methods she can. She's most interested in making a garment quickly and well—one that will stand up under lots of hard wear.

A grandmother or doting aunt, on the other hand, is more inclined to make a stylish little dress with fine embroidery or applique and loving attention to detail.

Whether you do it the fast and easy way, or slowly and with meticulous care, sewing for children can be rewarding and lots of fun.

Types of fabrics

Use easy-care fabrics—blends of man-made fibers that shed soil and wrinkles, need little or no ironing, or use natural fibers treated to give the same properties. Fabrics should also be soft, pliable, and have some absorbency. Colors should be colorfast, and the patterns relatively small.

Selecting a pattern

Never use age as the deciding factor in selecting a pattern for a child. Children the same age differ widely in height, weight, and build. Choose the pattern according to the breast measurement for a girl and the chest measurement for a boy. A short, chubby girl of 6 may need a size 8 pattern, while a tall, thin six-year-old may take only a size 4 pattern. Both would probably need adjustment in length; these changes are easier to make than altering a whole pattern.

Measurements

INFANTS AND TODDLERS

Size	½	1	2	3
Breast	19	20	21	22
Waist	19	19½	20	20½
Dress length (at center back)	13½	14½	15½	16½
Arm length	9	10	11	12

CHILDREN

Size	4	5	6	7	8
Breast	23	23½	24	25	26
Waist	21	21½	22	22½	23
Hip	—	25	26	27	28
Back length (neck to waist)	9	9½	10	10½	11
Arm length	14⅛	15⅛	16⅛	16⅞	17⅝
Over-all length	Shown on pattern envelope				

GIRLS

Size	7	8	10	12	14
Breast	25	26	28	30	32
Waist	22½	23	24	25	26
Hip	27	28	30	32½	35
Back length (neck to waist)	11	11½	12¼	13	13¾
Arm length	16⅜	17⅛	18⅝	20⅛	21⅜
Over-all length	Shown on pattern envelope				

After you have selected the right size pattern, take the child's measurements and compare them with the chart that's printed on back of pattern envelope (see illustration).

When taking a child's measurements, hold the tape measure snug, with a finger between tape measure and body. The pattern allows all the necessary ease. Here are the measurements you need to take with the tape.
Chest: Carefully measure around the fullest part of the chest.
Waist: Take a snug measurement at the exact natural waistline of child.
Hips: Needed only for pants. Measure at the fullest part of the hips.

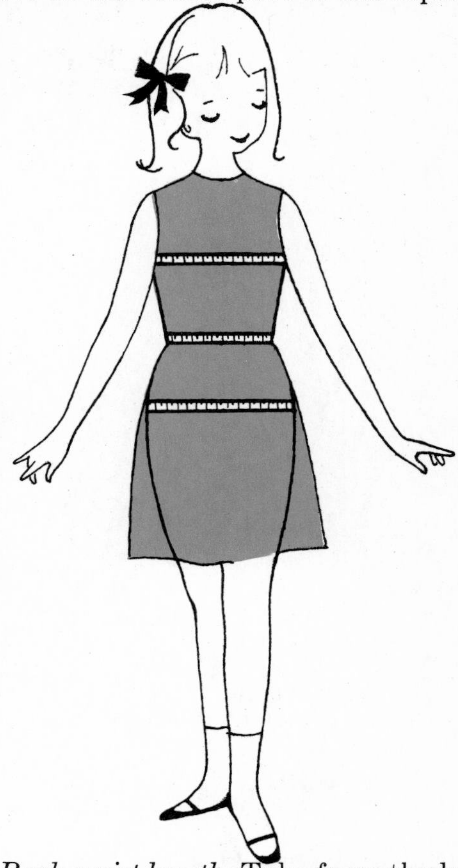

Back waist length: Take from the base of the neck to the waistline.
Front waist length: Measure from the base of the throat to the waistline.

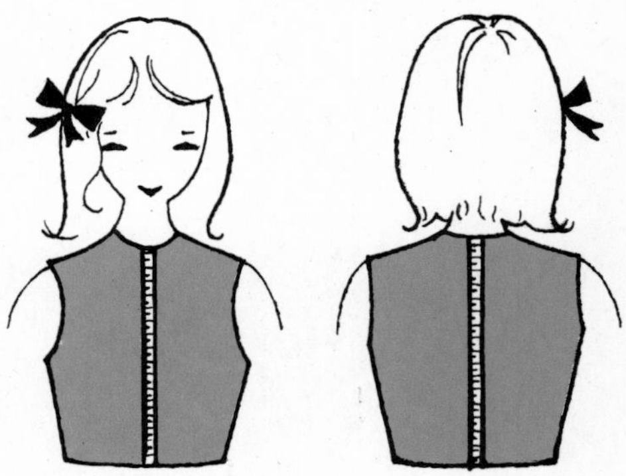

Garment length: Take in back from the waistline to the finished hemline of the skirt, or from the side waist to the finished length of the pants.

You can compare most of these measurements with those shown on the pattern envelope. These added ones make it easier to alter pattern.

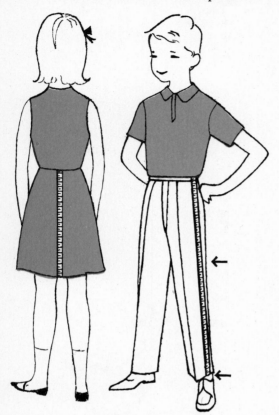

Back, front shoulder width: Take from armhole seam to armhole seam, 2½ inches down from base of throat.
Top of shoulder: Measure the shoulder from the neckline to the point where the sleeve sets into armhole.

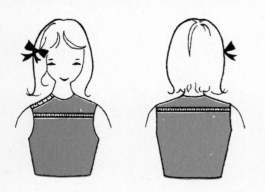

The pattern can be adjusted from measurements alone. Adjustments on a child's pattern are much easier to make than on an adult pattern.

Take out all the pattern pieces you need for the dress style you are making. If the pattern waist is smaller than the child's measurement, divide the amount you need by four. Add this amount to each side of back and front pattern pieces before you cut.

If the pattern has a 22-inch waist,

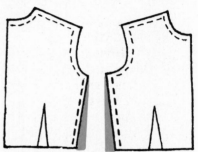

for instance, and your child measures 24 inches, you'll need to add 2 inches. Divide the two inches by four, which equals ½ inch. You would add ½ inch to each side seam on the back and front pattern pieces to increase the garment's waistline 2 inches.

Compare and adjust hip measurement the same way. It isn't necessary to measure pattern at these points.

With the exception of the back waist length, which is shown on the measurement chart, you will need to

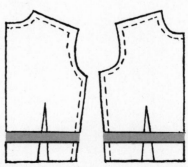

compare all other measurements by measuring the actual pattern. Compare child's measurement to this measurement. To lengthen, slash the pattern between the waist and breast and spread. Lengthen both front and back waist pieces the same amount.

Shorten the pattern with a tuck at the same point. Now, compare skirt length with the pattern. Lengthen or shorten the skirt length at the bottom of the skirt pattern piece.

Measure the back and front shoulder widths on the pattern pieces at the same points you measured on the child. Compare with child's measurements. If there is only a slight difference between the two, it is not necessary to adjust the pattern.

Check the top of the pattern shoulder measurement with the measurement taken on the child. If it has to be altered at the top of the shoulders as well as at the armhole seam, ad-

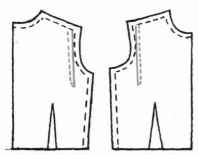

just the shoulders. Narrow shoulders with tuck from the top of shoulder toward chest, as on a woman's dress.

To make the shoulder wider, slash

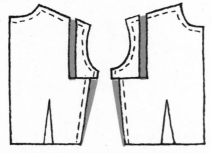

pattern across under armhole to center of shoulder. Spread the necessary amount. Make all adjustments in pattern first. Lay out, then cut.

Fitting the dress

Take the cut-out pattern, one piece at a time. Mark all darts, tucks, or gathers; sew them and other detail by machine. There's little danger of having to rip out any stitching.

Join the back and front waist. Sew up the underarm of the sleeve. For a puff sleeve, sew the gathers at either end. Shirr the sleeve to fit the armhole. Baste it into the dress.

You can shirr the other end of the sleeve to the approximate size, but leave the shirring threads loose so the sleeve can be adjusted to fit.

Sew up the seams of the skirt and gather the top of the skirt, as for any shirred skirt. Gather skirt to fit the waist size; then baste the skirt and the waist together.

The dress is now ready for fitting. There are no pins in it to stick or scratch, so a child won't mind the fitting. Pin the dress in place. Then check the fit of the garment.

Check the width of the shoulders. Make a note of the amount to add or to take in. Pinch in the amount that shoulders need to be narrowed and make a note. If the shoulder is too narrow, rip out the sleeve basting and check amount the shoulder can be let out. Correct when dress is off.

Tie a belt around the waist to check the waist length. If it drops below the belt, the waist needs to be shortened. If it rides up over the belt, it needs to be lengthened. Note the adjustment needed. Sometimes the entire bodice may be too large. Pinch a tuck the length of the waist to see how much it should be taken in. You can make this alteration easily after dress is off. Measure the hem, then turn it up for the correct length.

Now check the sleeve. If it is much too loose, shirr it to the right size with a gathering thread. Tie thread to the correct size. Then the dress can be unpinned and removed. Make all the alterations on the pattern and re-cut the dress to the altered pattern.

If the waist was too large, fold a tuck the length of the pattern, folding the amount measured. Then, re-cut the dress to fit the altered pattern.

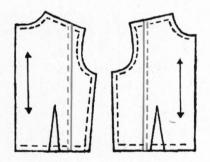

If the waist was too long, recut it to the correct length. Or, leave the extra length for a let-out tuck in the waistline seam for future alterations.

Don't cut away the extra fabric in the skirt length. Instead, leave a deep hem so the skirt can be lengthened for additional months of wear as the child grows taller.

As you can see, there is very little fitting necessary if the pattern is altered to the child's measurements before it is cut. If you buy the pattern according to breast size, it will fit the child correctly, whether she is slightly chubby or is thin.

Only the length of the garment will need adjusting. The neckline and the armholes will fit correctly, with no need for alteration.

Letting out seams

Most children seem to shoot up in height before they gain weight. Allowing for this sudden growth is no problem when you use let-out seams on the garments that you sew.

Let-out bodice tuck

As you cut the bodice, allow from 1½ to 2 inches on the length of the bodice for a let-out tuck. Add this extra length to the corrected pattern.

If it's necessary to add 1 inch to the waist length for your child, for example, add an additional 1½ inches for a let-out tuck. Join the skirt to the waistline, taking only a ⅝-inch seam. Then, just above this seam, take a ¾-inch-deep tuck on the inside of bodice. Sew it on the sewing machine, using a large stitch that can be ripped easily. Press the tuck up.

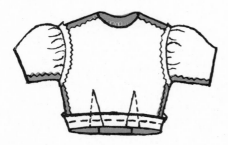

Make up the top of the dress just as you would if the tuck was not there. Be sure not to catch the tuck in any trimming or finishing detail, so that when you rip it open to lengthen the waist, it is not sewed in with any finishing. The amount the waistline can be lengthened later depends on how deep you make the let-out tuck when you make the garment.

Let-out skirt tuck

As you cut the skirt, add several inches on the length in addition to the amount needed for a full hem, or to give greater length for the tall child. Turn the hem at correct length and press the hemline all around.

Before you sew the hem, make a deep tuck close to the edge of the hem, taking up all the extra length added to the skirt. Sew it with a large stitch by machine. Finish the hem by hand, and press tuck toward hemline.

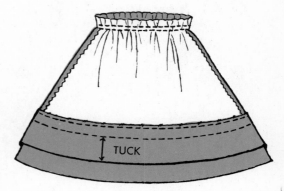

TUCK

You can make the tuck as deep as you like, as long is it doesn't hang below the hem edge. If you want to let the hem down 2 inches, for instance, it isn't necessary to rip out the hem. Simply sew the tuck 2 inches in from the original stitching line. The fold line of the hem will drop 2 inches without having to rip out the hem.

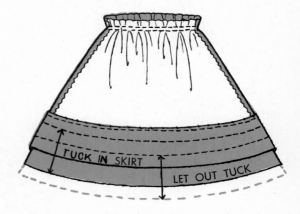

TUCK IN SKIRT

LET OUT TUCK

Shoulders

Shoulders seldom need to be made wider, but if you want to allow a let-out seam at the shoulder, you can cut the shoulder of the dress 1 inch wider than the pattern calls for.

Slash the pattern from the top of the shoulder toward the waist. Spread 1 inch. Sew up the bodice of the dress, then set in the sleeve. Take a tuck on the inside of the dress along the armhole for about 2½ inches toward the back and the front.

This tuck releases the fullness toward the breast, but the stitching over the shoulder holds the fullness in place so the shoulders aren't too wide.

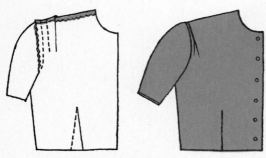

It also gives softness to the dress. When the shoulder needs to be widened, the tuck, which has been sewed with a large stitch on the machine, can easily be ripped out. As the tuck is made narrower, the shoulders become wider. The ½-inch let-out tuck in each shoulder allows you enough fabric so you can enlarge the shoulders 2 inches when necessary.

Let-out waistline

Many pattern companies make children's dresses with an elasticized waistline across the back. The waistline expands as the child grows.

If your pattern does not have this feature, it is easy to add it. When you cut out the bodice pieces, add a little extra fabric on the side seam of the back bodice. Don't sew up the back darts. On a shirred skirt, shirr the back skirt to the exact size of back bodice. If the skirt is fitted, cut the back skirt larger to match the back bodice. If the skirt has darts, don't sew the back skirt darts. Instead, join the skirt and the waist together with a regular inside seam.

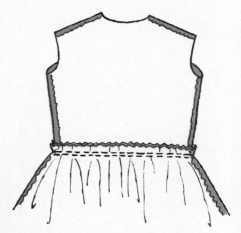

Use a 1-inch commercial bias binding. Unfold it and sew one edge along the back waistline on the seam allowance line. Sew the other edge to the bodice to form a casing. Draw a ¾-

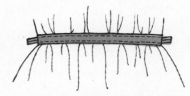

inch elastic through the casing so the waistline fits snug. Tack the elastic at the side seams where the casing ends. (See the illustration below.)

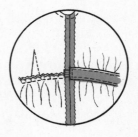

Seams

On most children's dresses you can use an inside seam. French seams are better for very lightweight or sheer  fabrics, except at armholes, where French seams are never used. On a lightweight fabric, stitch the armhole seam second time, 1/4 inch from the original armhole seamline and trim.

On a sheer fabric, stitch the armhole seam a second time. Trim and whip the raw edge, as you would do on any sheer dress fabric.

On fabrics like organdy that are both sheer and crisp, seams have a tendency to irritate a child's tender skin. To avoid this, spread the armhole seams. Turn the edge of each seam toward the inside. Overcast the folded edges together. This makes a fine, hand-turned French seam.

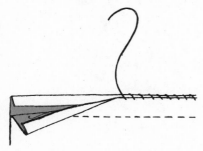

Another seam used for the same purpose is the hemmed-over seam. Trim away one side of the seam. Fold over the untrimmed seam and hem it over other at seam allowance line.

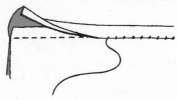

Neckline finishes

Necklines on children's clothes are either bound with bias or are finished with a collar. It's important to keep the neckline from stretching, since this can cause the dress to set badly.

Too large a neck or a sleeve that's too wide makes a child look thin, and the dress look too big. When you purchase your pattern by child's chest measurement, the armhole and neck size are almost always correct.

Run a stay-stitch around the neckline to hold it in shape. Then, check it with the neck size of the pattern. If the neckline has stretched, ease it in to the pattern size.

It isn't necessary to interface the collar on a child's dress. It is better to keep it soft and pliable.

Collar

Cut upper and under collar. Set any ruffling or trimming in the seam as you sew the collar together.

Lace or eyelet should be ruffled before it is applied to the collar so it will shape to the curve of the collar edge. Many of these trims come already ruffled and are easy to apply.

Sew the edge of the ruffling along the edge of the upper collar on the right side. Taper the ruffling to a point at the ends of the collar.

Contrasting cording in a collar edge is a popular trimming. (For complete

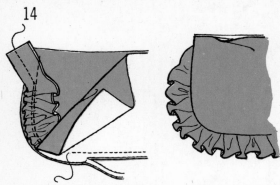

instructions on how to make cording, see page 17.)

Gathered neck

A soft, gathered neck is popular on dresses for children. It is always finished with a bias binding. Most patterns furnish you with a guide piece that shows you the size to which the neck should be shirred.

On sheer fabrics, the neck is shirred just to the size of the guide. Otherwise, the guide piece can be cut out of the fabric and then used as a stay. Put the wrong side of the stay to the inside of the dress and shirr the neck to fit. Sew this stay into place. Cut

and press the bias binding as shown on page 16. Sew the binding to the neckline on the right side, stretching it slightly as you sew.

Start at the shoulder, where piece-

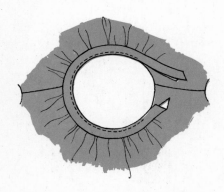

ing is done, and leave a 2-inch end loose. Then, sew all around neck to about 4 inches from where you began

stitching. Carefully measure and match the bias on straight grain. Sew the bias together so that it is continuous at this point. Now press the seam open. Press again on the original fold. Stitch this small section to the neck edge. The bias should al-

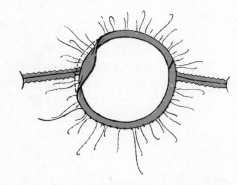

ways be joined this way at the neckline, sleeves, and wherever a continuous binding is needed. Never lap at a joining. This gives a bulky look. Fold bias over seam; sew fold edge by hand along original seamline.

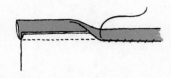

Making ruffling

The softest ruffling is made on the bias. It can be cut in strips and then hemmed. Most professionals make their ruffling on a double fold.

Cut the bias twice the width, plus seam allowance. Press in half on the length. The trick is to sew the edges together first to prevent twisting when it is put through ruffler. All sewing machines have this attachment.

and then turned more professionally.

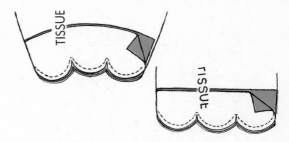

Scallops

Scallops are a favorite trim on children's clothes. They can be used at necklines, on collars, bandings, or at hems. To get the scallops even and well-shaped, make a tissue paper pattern. Trace the part of the dress pattern where you want to use the scallops. You can use a scalloping ruler to mark exact size of the scallops.

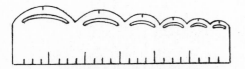

Figure the number and size of scallops that will evenly fit the space. Mark scallop design on the tissue.

Put the finished edge of the scallop along the seam allowance line. Pin

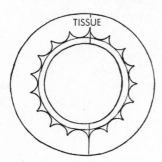

the facing to the dress, right sides together. Pin the tissue tracing over this. Sew through the tracing as you sew around each scallop. Take a single stitch across the base of each scallop, so that the corner can be clipped

Remove tissue. Trim around each scallop. Clip to stitching on curve, and well into each corner before turn-

ing it. When the facing is turned to the inside, run a fingernail around the inside of each scallop so it turns completely to give you a full, round shape. Then press the scallops, working with care.

Finish as you would for any facing. If an interfacing is needed, use the nonwoven type and mark the scallops on it. Cut away the seam allowance all around each scallop. Sew along the edge of each scallop when you are sewing it to the facing.

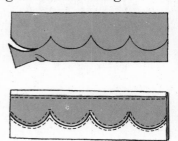

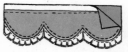

Stitch just outside each scallop when sewing the facing to the dress. To finish, trim, turn, and press as described above.

Bias

Bias is made by cutting fabric on the diagonal grain. This creates greater elasticity, which permits the bias to be used in more ways than a straight piece of fabric. It must be cut on the true bias, however, or it will twist and pull and be hard to use. Many home sewers find it hard to use home-made bias, but have no difficulty with commercial bias. This professional trick will help you make a binding from self-fabric which is as easy to use as a commercial one.

Bias binding

To get a true bias, fold material so crosswise thread runs parallel to the lengthwise thread, or selvage. Mark width you want with chalk. Cut bias strip twice the finished width, plus $\frac{1}{2}$ inch seam allowance. Join all bias pieces on length of goods. Fold bias

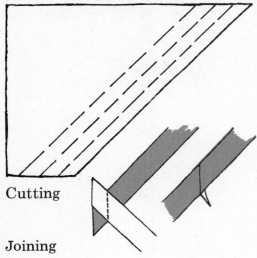

Cutting

Joining

on length and press. Trim edges so entire length of bias is even. Bias piece is now pressed, ready to use.

Roll binding (French piping)

Used on sheer fabrics or as a trim. Take pressed binding and sew raw edges to edges of garment, with right sides together. Trim seam to half the width of binding and roll fold edge over it. Tack in place just under the stitching line. When binding is used to finish a round neck, it should stay flat against neck and not ripple. Pin or baste a few inches of binding to neck, stretching it as you go. Roll to test for ripples. If correct, sew to neck, stretching in same way.

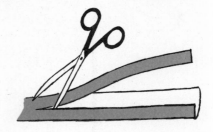

Bias facing

For a smooth, flat bias facing, trim one side of the bias off between the fold edge and raw edge. If bias is to

be used on a curve (around a neck, for example), curve bias to shape of neck with iron before applying.

Sew raw edge to neckline. Fold edge should be held flat to neck, as it will be when finished. Trim the neck seam and clip in every ½ inch along seam to stitching line. Turn bias to inside, press, slip-stitch in place.

Sewing a bias sash

Bias is easy to handle when you press and stretch it to form binding, or when you cut and sew it over cord to make cording. But, try to sew a bias fold of fabric for a sash, and it seems to twist and turn, no matter how carefully you sew it. Here is a professional trick that will insure a perfect sash, with no twisting.

Place fold of bias on the ironing board, right side out. Stretch and press on a fold. While it's stretched on board, clip seam at open edge of sash every 4 inches for entire length.

Remove from board and turn so the right sides are together, ready to sew the seam. As you sew, stretch seam, matching clip marks all along seam allowance. Leave about 4 inches open in center of seam. Turn to the

right side through this opening. Now baste along seamline to hold in place until it is pressed. Press lightly, then remove basting, and give it a final pressing. Slip-stitch the 4-inch opening together by hand.

Bias cording—piping

Children's fashions now feature popular self-binding and cording on necklines, pockets, and jacket edges.

To make cording, cut bias and cover the cording as you do for a cord buttonhole. Generally, the same ⅛-inch cording is used, so bias should be

1¼ inches. Occasionally, a heavier cording is used for a trim. The bias should then be cut wider; always have a ½-inch seam allowance.

If the cording is for use in the edge of a collar, then clip cording seam; sew cord to right side, with seam edges of collar and cording even. Pin facing directly to collar with the stitching line of cording showing on the collar side.

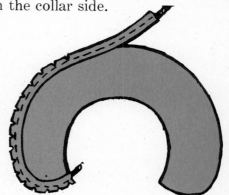

Sew upper and under collars together along this stitching line. Trim seam. On a round collar, notch it as

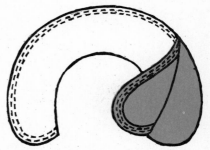

well. Turn collar to right side; cording will be in place, and seam flat and smooth. The same method is used for cording the seam of a garment. Sew cording to right side first so you can see that it is accurate. Then, permanently join cording by stitching along the original cord stitching line on the wrong side.

Sleeves

Be sure the sleeve is fitted fairly closely to arm size. If the sleeve is too big around, the child's arm looks thin. When making a puff sleeve, carefully shirr it to arm size.

If the sleeve edge has fitted band, you should make the band about 2 inches larger than the arm. A sleeve bound with bias should also be about 2 inches larger than the child's arm.

Sleeve band

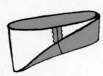

Cut the sleeve band from the pattern piece. Measure and sew the band to the correct size for child's arm. Press open the under-arm seam of band, press in half. Pin the band to the underarm seam of the sleeve, one edge of the band to the inside of the sleeve. Shirr the sleeve to fit the band. Smooth the

shirring so that it is even all around. Pin and sew the band to the sleeve. Sew on the shirred side of the sleeve. Press the seam into the sleeve band. Turn under the free edge of the sleeve band, and pin over the seam. Edge-stitch the band on the right side.

Bias binding

Press the bias on the length. Cut to the correct arm size, plus seam allowances. When you cut the bias to be joined, be sure to cut it on the straight grain. Join the bias, then press the seam open, and re-press the

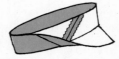

length fold. Pin both of the edges of the bias to the right side of the sleeve. Shirr the sleeve to fit the bias. Then carefully pin and sew the bias to the sleeve edge.

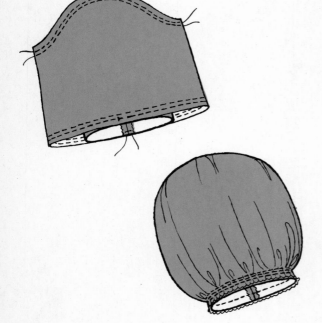

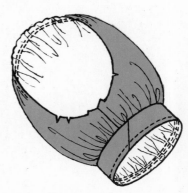

The sleeve can be finished by machine. Now trim the seam more than half the width of the bias. Fold the bias over the seam so the fold extends beyond the original stitching line. Turn to the right side. Sew by machine just under the fold edge of the bias. The neck of the garment can also be finished in this way.

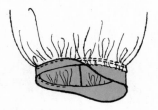

Ruffled sleeve with casing

A full, shirred sleeve can easily be made with a ruffled edge. Cut this sleeve 3 inches longer than you would cut a regular sleeve. Turn back a 2-inch hem. Turn under ¼ inch on the hem edge and pin and stitch to the inside of the sleeve. Measure down ⅝ inch from this stitching and then stitch a second row to form the casing. Cut a piece of ½-inch elastic 1 inch

smaller than arm girth. Draw through casing, lap ends, sew together.

If you want a fuller ruffle to the sleeve, sew the ruffle separately. Sew a piece of ruffling along the edge of the regular puff sleeve, right side of ruffling to right side of the sleeve.

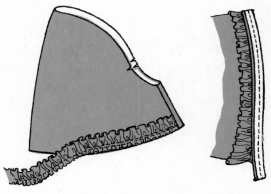

Sew the edge of a commercial bias binding along the same seam, sewing the right side of the binding along the ruffle. Turn the binding to the inside; stitch the loose edge of the binding to the sleeve for a casing. Draw the elastic through the casing and sew the ends together by hand.

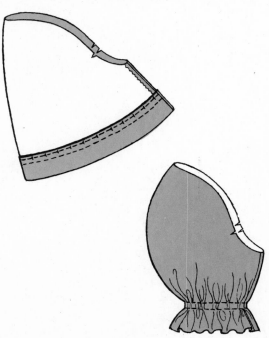

Skirt plackets

Zippers are seldom used in children's dresses. A placket is used when a child's dress opens down the back.

The back skirt may have a seam or be slashed. In either case, the placket of the skirt is easy to make.

Placket used with a seam

Sew up the back skirt seam to the

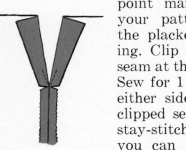

point marked on your pattern for the placket opening. Clip into the seam at this mark. Sew for 1 inch on either side of the clipped seam as a stay-stitch. Then you can trim off part of the seam width. To make the placket, cut a strip of fabric about 1½ inches wide and double the length of the placket opening. If possible, cut it along the selvage. Fold under the raw edge for ¼ inch and press it. Then fold on the length so the fold edge is just inside the selvage edge and press. Slide the placket piece over the seam, with the selvage edge on the under side. Pin in place. Then at the base of the placket opening, pin it so the fold edge is along

the stay-stitching. Stitch it on the right side along fold edge of placket piece, and the placket is finished. Use this method wherever a placket is needed on children's garments.

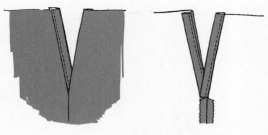

Slash placket opening

Mark where the placket is to be sewed. Sew a stay-stitch along the placket marks. Slash to the point of the stay-stitch. Fold and then press the placket piece as for the placket used with a seam. Slide the placket piece over the edges of the slash, making sure you catch placket piece along stitching line at lower point.

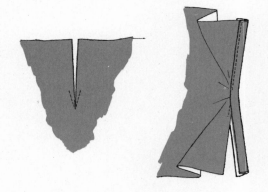

Pin and stitch along the fold edge, and the slash placket is finished.

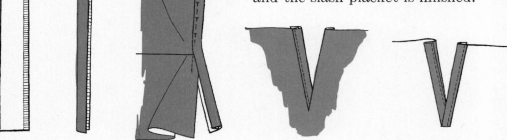

Hems

Turn under the skirt edge ½ inch and sew by machine on a straight skirt. Turn up the hem on the hem mark and press. Slip-stitch by hand, taking a back-stitch every few stitches to make the finished hem stronger.

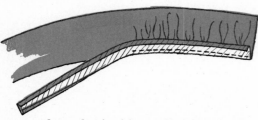

Use a commercial, flat-fold bias binding to hem a flared skirt. Unfold one edge and put it to the hem edge, right sides together. As you sew the bias binding, stretch it; the bias eases in the hem fullness. When the hem is

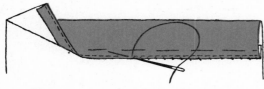

turned to the inside and pressed, the fullness adjusts itself to the inside of the skirt. Then slip-stitch the fold edge of the bias to the skirt and the hem is finished.

Lengthening a dress

Here are some simple and attractive ways to lengthen a dress, using self-fabric or trim of contrasting color.

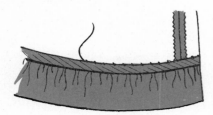

View 1

This style shows contrast used at the waistline of both skirt and bodice to lengthen them. Self-fabrics can be used in the same way, with pretty trimmings concealing the seams. Use lace, eyelet or other trimmings.

View 2

The illustrations shown at the bottom of the preceding page use contrast at the hem to lengthen the skirt. A yoke is also cut from it to lengthen the bodice. White organdy and lawn are good fabrics to use. Edged in lace or banding, they give a dainty trim effect to a dress. On heavier fabric, pique or linen can be used.

View 3

Contrast is used in bands to add to the skirt length. Bands can also be used in the bodice to give length. This dress could also be made with a bodice that has a contrasting yoke. A strip of fabric (tucked self-fabric, for instance) could be set in between the bands, with the bands used only as trim and the inset adding length.

Designing children's clothes

After you have made a few children's dresses, you may want to try your hand at designing or styling some yourself. The basic body lines that you find on children's dresses are simple. For example:

The *basque or the dirndl* type is a fitted bodice with a full skirt.

The *empire line* is actually a short-waisted version of the basque. This gives the garment a high yoke effect.

The *princess line* is a fitted and gored dress with simple styling.

The *A-line* was used in children's clothes long before Dior introduced it in fashions styled for adults.

The *dropped waistline* can be a version of any of the other styles. You create it by the way you cut the dress.

When you look over children's dresses you'll see how many of them are based on these few body lines. By adapting them, and by using your own ideas for the trimmings and embroidery detail, you can make charming and individual clothes.

Add a blouse or a skirt pattern, a jacket and slacks pattern; there is no limit to the wide variety of clothes you can make for a young lady.

Style features can be interchanged on these five basic body lines. For instance, a princess style can be cut off at the hipline and a pleated skirt added for an entirely new look.

Any of these styles can be adapted to make a popular jumper. Simply cut the armhole slightly deeper, and then shape the neck lower to show the collar line of an attractive blouse.

Five basic styles of dresses

Combine or vary these basic body lines for pretty, original little-girl fashions.

Basque or dirndl

Empire line

Princess line

A-line

Dropped waistline

Peter Pan collar
Short sleeve

2-piece Peter Pan
Puff sleeve

Tie collar
Shirt sleeve

Basic collars – sleeves

Collars

You can also assemble basic collar patterns. The four basic types shown here will give you a good selection.

You can make any other collar pattern pieces as you need them.

Sleeves

When you study patterns, you'll find that there are only four styles of sleeves used in little girls' dresses. Other styles are actually variations of one of these basic types.

Assemble patterns for each of these basic sleeve types and keep them on hand to use as you style different dresses for your little girl.

Bias roll collar—¾ sleeve

Where to find design ideas

Look first for ideas in pattern books. They not only show all the latest children's fashions, but also provide basic pattern styles you'll want to start you on your own designing.

Many patterns are also sketched to show the use of contrasting fabrics, as well as braid, eyelet trim, binding, and self-fabric trims. Checks and plaids are also shown. These fabrics can be used in imaginative ways.

Next, look to the ready-to-wear market for inspiration. Check the children's departments of local stores, shop windows, and magazine and newspaper advertisements for ideas.

Trimmings departments will also provide ideas. Bright new braids, and edgings often inspire a design.

Fabrics departments, of course, will give you dozens of ideas, plus the lovely materials to carry them out.

Adapting patterns to other styles

The basque-type bodice serves as a master pattern. It's from a pattern such as this that several others are cut. It can be used to make an empire dress, or one with a high yoke. Boleros, plastrons, blouses, and even shirts can also be cut from this one pattern. And, you needn't be an expert pattern-maker to vary the master pattern to fit your own needs.

Making a pattern

If you want to convert a basque-type dress to an empire style, for example, you should first measure down from the front neck of the child to the depth of the waistline that you want for the empire style.

Measure to the same point on the pattern and then draw a line straight across the bodice. Add $5/8$ inch seam allowance before you cut.

Now decide on the style of skirt, neck, and the sleeve you want to use. It's a good idea to have a sketch of the style of dress that you want to make. It need not be a complete sketch—only enough detail is necessary so that it shows placement and proportion of each special feature.

It's easy to convert a basque dress to a trim empire-line style.

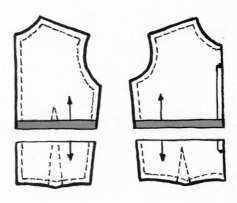

Empire bodice

This style has an empire bodice that opens down the back. There is a band with a ruffle trim down the front, and a ruffle trim at the neck. The style has a straight shirred skirt and short puff sleeves. (See page 21 for two other sleeves of this type.) There's also a ruffle used at the joining of the skirt and bodice. Make ruffling as shown on page 14, or if you wish you can use commercial ruffling.

On the back bodice of this style, add ¾ inch to extend the back, and also add 3 inches for the facing.

The simple skirt is made of only two lengths of fabric that are shirred to fit the bodice. On this type of dress, where the fullness is not as much as in the basque style, skirt fullness will be approximately 2 or 2½ to 1. For example, if the lower edge of the bodice measures 24 inches, the skirt will be from 48-60 inches wide, depending on the fullness you want.

Cut one piece for the front skirt on a fold. Also cut the back skirt on a fold, but make a slash in the back for an opening, then finish with a lapped zipper application for a neat closure.

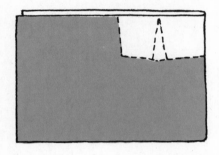

Cut the band for the front of the dress about 1½ inches wide, plus the seam allowances. Apply the ruffling on either side. Press the seam allowances back, then pin, and sew the band to the front of the bodice.

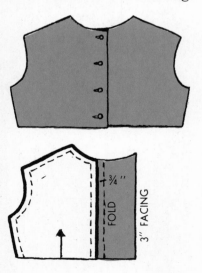

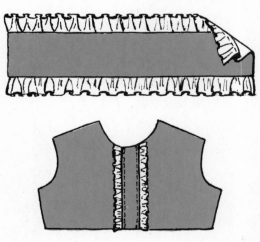

By using the same bodice type,

with a change of skirt and sleeve, you can make innumerable styles. With only a few minor changes, for example, you can use the pattern that you have just finished to make a pinafore or jumper. Simply eliminate the sleeve. Cut the neckline deeper in either a square or scoop neck style. Open the back skirt, as well as the bodice, and add pockets. Make a pinafore slightly shorter than the dress; use the dress length for a jumper.

If you wish, you can use many other skirt styles with this bodice.

Shaped or flared skirt

Here's how you can make many additional skirt styles. Take the lower bodice piece that was cut off when you made the empire top. Place this pattern on a piece of tissue paper, fold edge of lower bodice along an edge of tissue paper. Mark the seam allowance at the top. Then measure the length of the skirt on the fold edge and mark point on the tissue.

Now at the top of the tissue, measure the width of the bodice piece, from the fold edge to the outside edge. Measure same distance at hemline and draw a line between these points for the length of the tissue pattern. At the hemline, measure out an added 4 inches beyond this line and mark it. Now draw a line from the waistline mark to this hem mark, and you will have a shaped skirt.

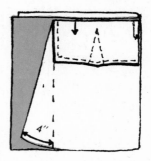

You can make many skirt variations from this skirt pattern. For instance, here are four styles, all of them with the same bodice treatment and shaped skirt; yet each has a different look because of a change in the pleating used in the skirt. You can make all of these skirts easily, using your shaped skirt pattern.

View 1

To make dress shown at bottom of page 27, make tissue tracing of the shaped pattern. Add piece of tissue 6 inches wide to front or fold edge of skirt piece. At top of skirt, measure in 3 inches on tissue and mark. At hemline, mark tissue 6 inches from front line. Draw a line from top mark to hem, to indicate new front line of skirt. Fold along original front line and lap to new line, forming an inverted pleat at front. While pleat is folded in, cut off excess tissue at skirt

View 2   View 3

inches at hem. Draw a line from waist to hem at these points. Slash pattern

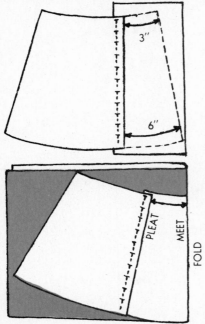

on this line. Spread 4 inches at the waist and 6 inches at hem. Insert tissue to form pleat. Fold in pleat, trim

front. When cutting, lay new front line on a fold of fabric. If fabric is too narrow, add seam allowance and cut skirt in two pieces with a seam at center of pleat inlay. Use back skirt shown at bottom of page 27. Make a 4-inch flare at center back to make two-piece back skirt.

View 2

Trace shaped skirt pattern on tissue. To form box pleat in this style, measure from fold line where pleat will go; measure 2½ inches at top and 4

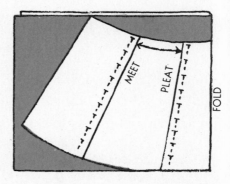

at top and hem to form pattern. Use 2-piece back skirt with this front.

View 3

This style is made in almost the same way as View 2, except that the pleat on each side is an inverted one. Allow slightly more width for the inlay of the pleat—about 4 inches at the waist and 8 inches at the hem. Fold each pleat to meet in the center of the inlay, forming an inverted pleat with a flare for the skirt.

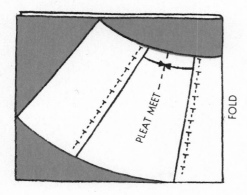

View 4

This skirt is sewed from straight lengths of fabric, as you do for a shirred skirt. Decide on the number of pleats you want at front and back. You'll need to figure size of waistline, number of pleats, and the amount of overlay for each. To do this, go back to the original dress pattern from which you cut your flared skirt pattern. Ordinarily, you would use waist size to figure size of pleats, but since this skirt has a high empire line, with the pleats beginning at the chest, you will need to use the chest measurement to figure for the pleating. For example, on a size 6 pattern, the chest measurement is 24 inches. If you want four pleats in front and back, you would divide 24 inches by 8; each of the box pleats in the skirt would be 3 inches wide.

The underlay should be $1\frac{1}{2}$ inches, or 3 inches to form half a pleat. (See illustration.) On 36-inch fabric, you would have to skimp on each underlay for seam allowances.

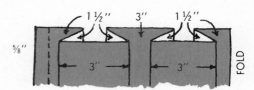

A-line styles

There has always been an A-line, or a flare-from-the-shoulder-type dress. Now it is being used in the new and flattering styles for children. These chic dresses compare with the smartest grown-up look, yet suit the very young. Two sketches at lower right, page 29 show versions of the style.

Both of these versions make good basic patterns from which you can create several other pretty variations.

View 1

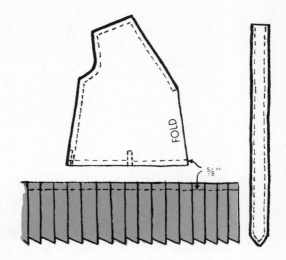

place last two on either side of back.

If you add shirt-style sleeves, the basic sailor dress will take on an entirely new and different look.

View 2

Buy a basic sailor dress pattern and then use it to make two new dresses with the same smart naval theme.

Take sailor pattern and measure up from the hem for about 8 inches. Cut off pattern at this line. Make a strip of pleating that's the same depth as the amount cut off the hem. Use a box pleat, as shown for the empire dress, or use side pleating.

Measure the lower edge of the dress and then figure the amount of pleating you need. Figure for the pleating as shown in the illustration on page **29**. After you have made the pleating and sewed it to form the hem of the dress, make a narrow belt and also some belt loops. Sew the belt loops (six are adequate) just over the pleating—one loop on either side seam, one on either side of the front;

In this variation, the basic sailor needs only to button down the front to achieve a new coat-dress styling. Add a facing to the front and button the dress from the collar to hem.

For still another version, leave off the sleeves and add pockets and a blouse to make a jumper.

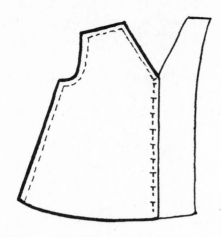

Making an A-line pattern

The second dress shown at bottom of page 29 is an almost perfect basic for the A-line. You can use it to make many styles in this category.

Make a tissue paper tracing of the front and back pattern. Draw a line from the center of the shoulder to the hem. Slash along this line. Insert a strip of tissue 6 inches wide where the pattern is spread. Cut out the dress. Fold so that an inverted pleat is formed on either side. Then stitch 1

inch from the edge of the pleat; sew for about 6 inches down one side, to a point at the center of the pleat, and up the other side to form a decorative slot seam.

Use a puff or a ¾ sleeve, and a two-piece Peter Pan style collar. Button the dress down the back. This style makes a charming little girl's dress. You can also make it with a center-front pleat as well. Pleats can be sewed on the inside.

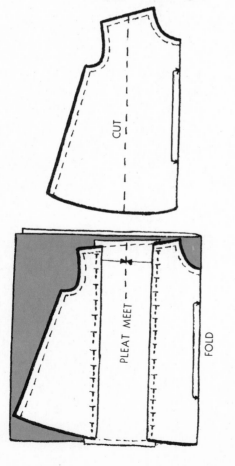

As you can see, you can create any number of original dresses with only simple changes. In addition to the style changes, the many choices of fabrics and trimmings provide an endless selection. You need never repeat a design unless you wish to.

Dropped-waist styles

Here are some dropped-waist styles, all taken from one pattern. Work out some of these ideas or improvise your own. The two below feature a tiered

ballerina skirt (left), and a demure high-neck, long-sleeved style (right).

Styles shown above can be tailored for a tomboy or frilly and feminine.

Trimmings to make

There are dozens of trimming touches that can give an entirely different look to the most simple dress. Sometimes, it's only the effect of smart plaid or check used on the bias that turns a simple dress into one that's really original and stylish.

Styling details to make

Plastron fronts can easily be made from a basque pattern. These fronts are small bib-type panels, used in the front bodice. They can be separate pieces that are either lined or finished with binding or edging. They can button on, be tacked on, or even can be sewed to the bodice as part of the design of the dress.

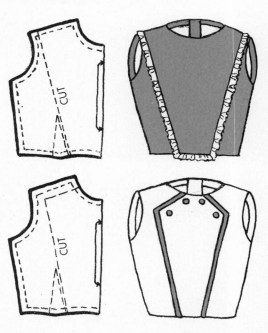

Boleros and weskits can also be cut easily from basque pattern. These can

Trimming details
cut on the bias

also be made as separate pieces or as a part of the dress.

The illustrations below show how bolero pieces can be cut and then sewed to the side and armhole of the dress to give the dress the finished effect of a separate, short jacket.

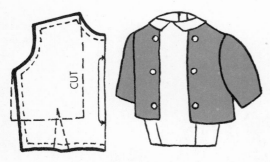

The illustrations below picture a weskit cut from the same bodice pattern. This is made up as a separate piece, and can be lined or faced as a finish. A weskit can be made in many

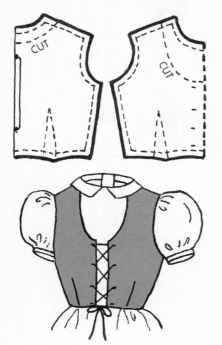

fabrics—in velveteen, polished cotton, corduroy, linen, or chintz. It can be worn over the fitted-bodice dresses, and even with some skirts and blouses. You might embroider the weskit in bright, pretty colors and use it for dress-up occasions.

Cording

Cording is often used as a trim on children's clothes. It is available in a variety of colors and textures, ready to sew. Or, you can make your own cording. See page 17 for instructions on how to make it.

Here are two other trims that are especially good for party dresses.

Beading

Beading is an insertion through which ribbon can be drawn. By substituting strips of self-fabric cut on the bias for the ribbon, you can also achieve a lovely effect. Beading is available commercially with the ribbon already threaded through it.

Ribbon and embroidered braid

Use these trimmings with lace edgings or with rickrack sewed along each edge to create a more colorful effect.

Pages 33 through 39 show many braids, edgings, rufflings, and applique ideas that can also be used effectively for interesting styling detail.

There is an endless variety of trimmings, all made up and ready to apply. Look for these colorful embroidered motifs, braids, and bandings in the trimmings department.

Applique accents are ready-to-sew

Perky dress trims

Make your own appliques

Trace, cut to actual
    size. Sew by hand in a
contrasting pattern.

Finishing detail

Fastenings

Buttons used on children's clothes should be washable. Pearl, bone, and plastic buttons are washable and colorfast, so they do not have to be removed from clothes before washing.

Zippers are also washable, and can be used in many places on children's clothes. Dot snap fasteners are practical, particularly for very young children. These fasteners come in kits, are hammered into the cloth.

Another type of fastening is made of nylon. In tape form, it has hooks on one side, loops on other side that interlock when pressed together.

You'll find all of these types of fasteners available in the notions department of a department store.

Embroidery stitches

Embroidery and applique are attractive on children's clothes. They can be done by hand or with a zigzag sewing machine. It's possible to do a great variety of stitches on these machines. Sewing machine companies offer instructions on how to make many types of special stitches.

Hand embroidery can be as simple or elaborate as you care to make it. Some women are very expert at handwork and find great pleasure in doing exquisite work. If you are unfamiliar with embroidery, start on a project that calls for simple, easy stitches.

Outline-stitch

Work from the left to right. Bring the needle out on the line, and take a short back-stitch. Keep your thread under the needle, bringing the needle

out where the last stitch went in. Continue this way to outline the design. Keep all stitches same length.

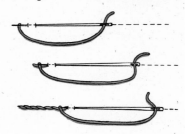

Satin-stitch

Pass your needle over, then underneath the fabric. Keep stitches close together so they fill in the design. To give a padded look, design should first be filled in with tiny running-stitches. Satin-stitch over these.

Chain-stitch

Bring the needle and thread to the right side of the fabric. Hold the thread to form a loop. Then insert the needle at the same point where the thread was brought through. Bring it out a short distance ahead to form the loop. Keep loops the same size.

Feather-stitch

Bring the needle up through the material on the design line. Take a short slanting stitch on the right side of the material, pointing needle to left or right. Hold the thread down with the thumb to form the loop. Take the next stitch on the opposite side of the line, pointing the needle the opposite direction. Continue this way, keeping all stitches the same length.

Blanket-stitch

Work from left to right with the edge to be blanket-stitched toward you. Mark the line for the depth of the blanket-stitch. Bring the thread to the right side of the fabric on this line.

Hold the thread with the thumb and bring the needle through the line on the right side of the fabric and out over the thread at the edge, forming a loop. The space between stitches can be any width you want. The length of the stitch can be varied to give you an assortment of stitches.

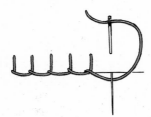

Lazy-daisy stitch

This basic stitch is the same as the chain-stitch. Each individual loop is worked from a center point. After each loop is finished, return the needle to the same point and continue to the next loop. Be sure to make the lazy-daisy stitches the same length.

French-knot

Bring the needle to the right side at the point where the knot is to be made. Point the needle in the same direction as the thread. Wind the thread around the needle two or three times. Push the needle back through the fabric at the point where the first stitch was taken. Then pull the thread through to the wrong side, forming the knot.

Cross-stitch

Work from the left to right. Bring the needle through the fabric at the lower left-hand corner. Insert the needle at the upper right-hand corner of the cross and bring it under the fabric and out at the lower left-hand corner of the next stitch.

Sew across the fabric, making all of the stitches in one direction, crossing all the stitches. Keep the stitches together at both the top and at the bottom of each cross-stitch.

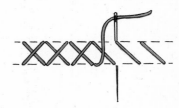

Applique

This is a method of applying one piece of fabric over the other with either a fine slip-stitch or with a decorative stitch. Usually, the decorative stitch used is a blanket-stitch or a feather-stitch. Sometimes, the pattern contains a transfer pattern.

See pages 35, 38, 39 for applique

ideas. Also check children's coloring books or story books. Simply trace the designs. For hand applique, the design should be traced to the finished size, cut out, allowing ¼-inch seam · allowance. Run a machine-stitch just outside of this line.

Turn the seam allowance of the applique piece just inside the machine line. Pin or baste the piece in place. Sew it on with a decorative stitch.

For machine-stitching, the applique can be cut, allowing ¼-inch seam allowance. Stitch it in place with a fine zigzag-stitch on the applique line. Trim. Re-stitch raw edge and stitching line with a satin-stitch.

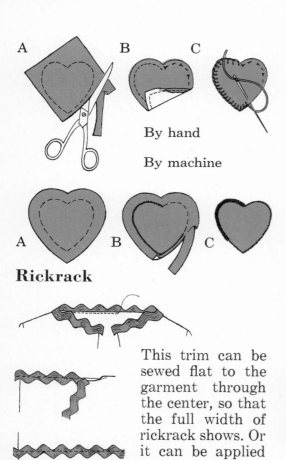

By hand

By machine

Rickrack

This trim can be sewed flat to the garment through the center, so that the full width of rickrack shows. Or it can be applied around edges so only one edge shows, with remainder of rickrack to underside of garment.

Smocking

There seems to be a revival in the art of smocking, especially for children's dresses. Ready-to-wear styles are also showing dresses with yokes, bodices, waistlines, and other shirred sections all done with hand-smocking. This treatment is a colorful trim, and is especially adaptable to smart party dresses for children.

You can buy patterns for smocking, prepared by commercial pattern companies. They offer color suggestions, as well as designs showing the combination of many stitches. A transfer pattern makes it simple to mark the garment for the position of the smocking. It is accurate and a big time-saver. If you are a beginner at embroidery or smocking, it's advisable to work from one of these commercial patterns. More experienced sewers can mark and figure their own stitches and design combinations.

Marking for smocking

Marking for smocking consists of a series of dots, evenly spaced across the right side of the fabric. On the light fabrics, dots should be about 3/16 inch apart. On heavier fabrics, dots can be spaced at ¼-inch intervals. A block of dots evenly spaced serves as a guide for most of the smocking stitches that you'll use.

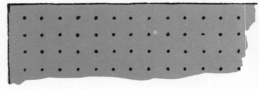

Special marking must be done when designs combine a variety of stitches.

Smocked yoke

Under yoke smocking

Design ideas for using smocking

Smocked bodice

Bodice smocking
with yoke

Neck and
sleeve smocking

In these instances, the commercial transfer patterns are very helpful. You can follow the designs already worked out for you, or can cut the transfers apart and arrange your own combinations for your design.

First, learn the variety of stitches that you'll use for smocking. Later in this section, you'll learn how to work out your own diagram, combine a number of stitches for interesting effect, and then mark the fabric.

Smocking stitches

When figuring fabric for smocking, fullness should be from 2½-3 to one. For example, if you want 12 inches of finished smocking, you would need from a 30-36 inch width of fabric.

Before you begin, familiarize yourself with the many smocking stitches and combinations in which they can be used. This is very important, since you can't mark your fabric for smocking until you decide what combination of stitches you want to use.

Picking up the stitch

There are two views on how a smocking stitch should be taken in relation to the dot. With the first method, work from right to left; insert the needle through the fabric halfway between the dots, and bring the needle out through the left-hand dot.

In the second method, work from the right to left, take the stitch under dot, an equal amount on either side.

Whichever method you decide to use, be consistent, and use it through-

out your entire piece of smocking.

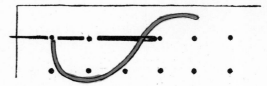

Gathering-stitch

The first row of dots is used for a gathering stitch, to shirr the fabric to fit the finished size of smocking.

You can use mercerized thread and a fine needle. Run a shirring thread from right to left, taking a stitch under each dot. Shirr to the finished size of the smocking. (This is done in conjunction with a smocking guide that is explained on page 47.)

Cable-stitch

Bring the needle through the first dot to the right side of the fabric. Take a stitch through the fabric under the second dot. Keep thread above the needle as you draw up the thread. Keep thread below the needle as you take a stitch under the third dot. On the fourth stitch, the thread is above the needle. Continue this way until the row is finished. Pull the thread either up or down, but always at right angle to the stitch. This helps to form more even folds.

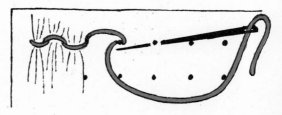

Outline-stitch

This stitch is used to hold the gathering-stitch first taken in the smocking. It is one of the easiest to do. Bring the thread through the first dot to the right side. Take a stitch under the second dot, but keep the thread above the needle as you draw up the thread. Continue this stitch to the end of the row. You can do a second row under the first row, but keep the thread under the needle as you draw up each stitch. This gives a smart herringbone effect.

It is a good idea to stretch the fabric lengthwise by hand as you complete each row. This stretching helps to straighten the folds.

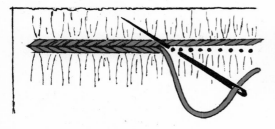

Honeycomb-stitch

Bring the needle through dot 1 to the right side of the fabric. Take a stitch under dot 2 and dot 1, and draw them together. Then take second stitch through the same dots and pull the thread taut. Insert your needle under the fabric at dot 2, and bring it out through dot 3. Take a stitch under dot 4 and dot 3, and draw them together. Take another stitch through the same dots and pull thread taut. Insert needle through dot 4 under the fabric, and bring it out through dot 5. Continue between the two sets of dots to the end of the row.

This stitch can be worked as deep as you like. Continue with the third and fourth rows, working them as you did for the first two rows.

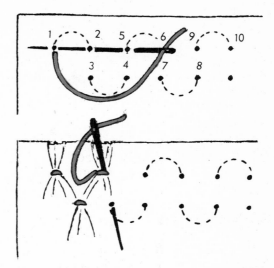

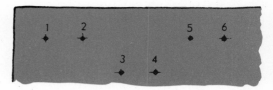

Wave-stitch

The diagram below shows the dot pattern for making the wave-stitch.

Bring the needle to the right side through first dot. Take a stitch under second, keeping thread above needle (A). Draw together by pulling thread down. With thread above needle, take a stitch under third dot (B). (See illustration on following page.) With thread below needle, take a stitch under fourth dot (C). Draw the stitches together by pulling thread up. With thread below the needle, take a stitch under the fifth dot (D). Keep thread over needle as you take stitch under sixth dot. Draw together by pulling thread down. Continue this way for the entire row.

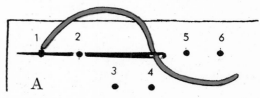

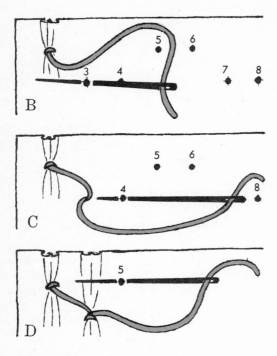

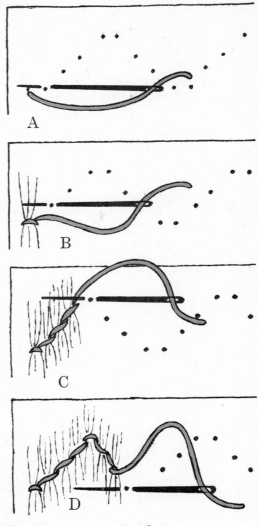

Three-step wave-stitch

Start at the fourth line and work up to form the wave-stitch. The diagram for this stitch is made up of eight dots. (See illustration below.)

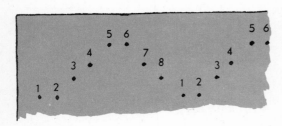

Bring needle through first dot at the left. Keep thread below the needle as you work up the wave. Pick up stitch under second dot. Draw together, pulling thread up (A). Pick up third, fourth, and fifth dots (B). Bring thread above needle as you pick up sixth dot. Draw fifth and sixth dots together by pulling thread down (C). Keep the thread above the needle as you pick up the three dots that are going down the wave (D).

Combining stitches

Many interesting effects can be created by combining smocking stitches. For example, the one-step wave can be used in two rows to create an attractive diamond-shaped pattern.

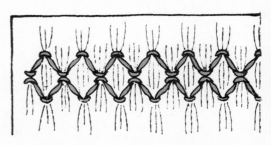

The cable-stitch can be used effectively with one-step, two-step, or with three-step wave-stitches.

By combining the cable-stitch with the wave-stitch, first running up, and then running down, the cable-stitch forms a flower effect, and the wave-stitch forms a diamond—an over-all design that is very pleasing.

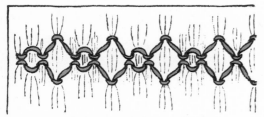

Cable-stitch and one-step wave

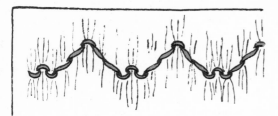

Cable-stitch and two-step wave

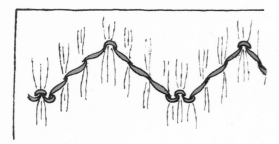

Cable-stitch and three-step wave

Whole bodices, yokes, and bandings, as well as trimming detail can be made by combining many different stitches to form blocks of colorful and beautiful smocking for dresses.

Making smocking guide

If you want an entire front bodice done in smocking, measure the width of your pattern at the widest part. Cut a straight piece of the dress fabric; cut three times the width and 2 inches longer than the pattern.

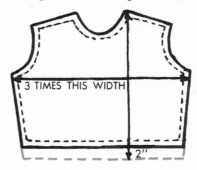

Cut the smocking guide out of heavy paper. Make it the same size as bodice pattern, plus 2 inches for seams and take-up of smocking.

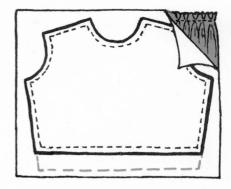

Mark the fabric for the smocking design. If you are not using a commercial transfer pattern, you will have to work out the design and mark your own. (See page 42.)

Gather the fabric along the first row of dots, as shown under "Gathering-stitch," page 44. Then gather the dress fabric to fit the top edge of the smocking guide. Baste the fabric to the guide along this edge. Also you should baste the side edges to the guide and the center of the fabric to keep it secure until the smocking is finished. Use six-strand embroidery cotton when you're smocking.

When smocking is finished, remove it from the smocking guide and steam press it lightly before cutting out bodice. Pin the top row of shirring to the ironing board. Hold the iron just above the fabric surface to let steam penetrate, as you gently stretch smocking slightly from the bottom. This will help form even pleats.

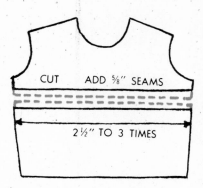

Cut the bodice pattern again from muslin or brown paper, but remove all of the seam allowances so you have a copy of the finished size. Lay this over the smocking. Be sure to line up the center of the bodice pattern with the center of the smocking. Also be sure the lower edge of the bodice is along the lower row of the smocking. Mark around neck, shoulder, armhole, side seam, and waistline seam on smocking. Mark with a

basting thread. Remove pattern; sew around the marked lines by machine.

Mark a $\frac{5}{8}$ inch seam allowance outside the stitching line and cut out the smocked bodice along this line. The dress can now be made up using the smocking piece to form the front bodice. It is not necessary to sew bodice darts into the smocking. It can be eased slightly at the waistline, instead of darting it.

If smocking is to be used under a yoke, measure the width of the bodice where it joins the yoke and cut your fabric 2½-3 times this width. Follow the same procedure for smocking and cutting as you do for whole bodice.

The best way to mark your fabric for smocking is with a transfer pattern, which many pattern companies make. Beautiful smocking designs are available with bandings of varying widths. You can use them exactly as the pattern shows, or cut them apart to form your own sequence of stitches.

If you need only straight blocks of dots for honeycomb or cable smocking, you can easily do this by machine.

Mark the lines for the dots on the wrong side of the fabric with tailor's chalk. Also mark a line down the left side of the fabric. Baste the fabric to be smocked to a piece of dressmaking carbon, right side of fabric against carbon side. Remove thread from the sewing machine. Adjust the stitch to the largest size (about 3/16 on most machines). Stitch along the chalk marks on the wrong side of the fabric, with the carbon between the fabric and sewing machine. Test first to be

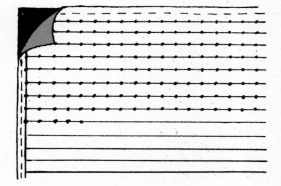

sure the pressure on the presser foot is not too heavy. If pressure is correct, you'll get a clear, clean dot, with no smudging of carbon. Adjust the pressure if needed.

To be sure the dots will line up, one under the other, always start the row of stitching by putting the needle down through the chalk line at the beginning of each line of sewing.

To make a pattern for a more complicated banding, get 3/16 to ¼ inch graph paper. Work out the design on the paper, using the corners of the squares on paper for the dots.

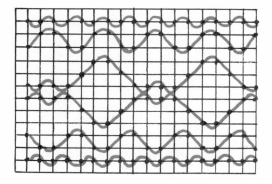

Fill-in

After the smocking is finished, other colors can be worked in by doing some fill-in rows. No additional marking is needed. This is done by filling in wide spaces either above or below the stitch with the same stitch, done in a contrasting color. Take the stitches

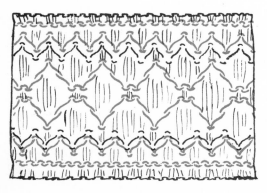

in the pleats formed by the original smocking row.

Machine smocking

The effect of smocking can be worked out by using embroidery over machine shirring. Do rows of shirring by machine at the point where you want the smocking effect. It is easy to shirr by machine. Enlarge the stitch on the machine, loosen the top tension and sew even rows of stitching to simulate smocking rows. Sew the shirring line on the right side of the fabric. Use the bobbin threads to shirr. When you do the shirring, ease as many rows as possible on bobbin threads at one time as you work.

After the shirring has been eased in, use the many varieties of embroidery stitches to give smocking effect.

You can use the same outline-stitch as you used for regular smocking.

Feather-stitching is also an excellent choice to use for a smocking stitch over shirring done on a machine.

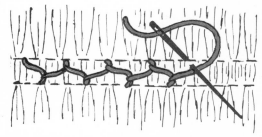

This stitch resembles wave-stitch in smocking. First, bring the needle to the right side through top stitching line of shirring. Take a stitch to the right; bring the needle out halfway between these stitches. Take a small stitch on the lower shirred line to the right of the top stitch. Then, take a stitch to the right, bringing the needle out at the same point of the down stroke of the first stitch. Continue working toward the right, first on the upper line of shirring, and then on the lower line of shirring.

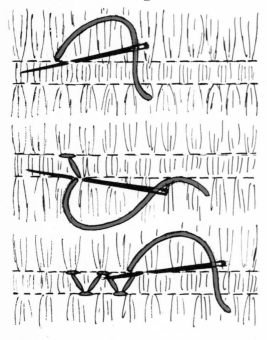

Many other variations of embroidery stitches can be used in the same way. It's a fast way to create a smocked effect without any difficulty.

Selection of fabric and colors

Smocking can be done on cottons, on silks, or sheer woolens. Solid-color fabrics look beautiful when they are sewed in contrasting thread, but don't limit yourself to only solid colors. Small calico prints are also very effective, with a smocking design that is done in colors of the print. Challis prints are also attractive when worked in smocking, with one or more colors used in the design.

Making coats

Children's coats are easy and fun to make as well as economical. One real economy factor—you can make the coat so it can be let out to "grow" with your child. And, you can choose the fabrics and colors that are most becoming and most long-wearing.

Coats can be made from many types of fabrics. If you want the coat to give good service for several years, choose a quality fabric equal to the workmanship you'll put into the coat.

Buy the same size pattern for the coat as for a dress. The pattern allows the necessary ease for linings and for wear over the other clothes. Don't buy too large a pattern, or the neckline and coat top will look too large on your child.

If any adjustments need to be made on the coat—such as lengthening the waist or narrowing the shoulders—make them in the pattern before cutting. Leave extra length on the hem and the sleeves so you can adjust coat in length as child grows.

All coats should be underlined. First cut all pattern pieces from the coat fabric, and then cut them in one of the lightweight, commercial underlining fabrics. Sew each individual piece of the coat to the underlining before assembling the garment. This is called "mounting" the coat.

Remove the pattern from the coat and mounting fabrics. Markings for the placement of pockets or other trim should be made on the right side of the coat pieces.

Put the wrong side of the coat pieces to the wrong side of the mounting fabric pieces and pin all around. Press pieces together. Re-pin if either layer shrinks. Sew pieces together all around, sewing just outside the seam allowance line. Mark any darts or tucks on the underlining.

Assembling the coat

Pin and sew all pieces of coat body together. Sew any darts or tucks. Sew up the sleeves, baste into armholes.

Press the seams carefully and try on the coat for size. There should be no alteration needed if you made the same adjustments that are necessary when you adjust a dress.

Do not overfit the coat. If the shoulders seem a little wide, it is better to put in a small pad, rather than to recut them. (Use a small pad, in any case, to give a better look through the shoulders.) Remember that the coat must fit over other clothing, so be sure there is plenty of ease. A box-type coat can be easier through the shoulders than a fitted, princess line because of its styling.

Mark for the hemline and length of sleeve while the coat is being tried on. Remove the coat and finish it.

Interfacing the coat

Interface the coat with hair canvas or a nonwoven interfacing. If the coat has a lapel, hair canvas is a better choice. Cut the interfacing so it is 1 inch wider than the facing and extends into the shoulder. This also

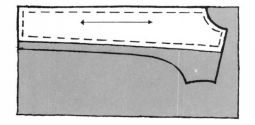

helps produce a better shoulder line. If the facings are attached to the coat, fold them back and press. Cut the front seam allowance off the in-

terfacing and pin the cut edge along the fold edge of the facing. Carefully catch-stitch the front edge along the fold line. Be sure that no stitches show on the right side.

Trim away the seam allowance around the neck of the interfacing and sew along the neck and the shoulder to about 2 inches from the armhole. Then catch-stitch the inside edge of the interfacing to the underlining of the coat. Make buttonholes.

The hem must be turned up before the facings can be finished to the inside of the coat. If the coat is underlined, baste the underlining and coat together at the hemline before turning up the hem. If the coat has an unusually deep hem (so it can be let down later), it is important that this depth of hem does not show on the right side. To prevent this, underline with an interfacing about 2 inches deeper than the hem.

On a box-type coat, there will be no shaping at the hem, so a straight piece of interfacing can be cut. If the coat is a princess-line style, the interfacing should be shaped to the flare of the coat. Pin the pattern pieces together turn back pattern hem at finished line. Place the pinned up pattern over underlining and cut interfacing piece from the pattern. Make interfacing piece 2 inches deeper than finished hem.

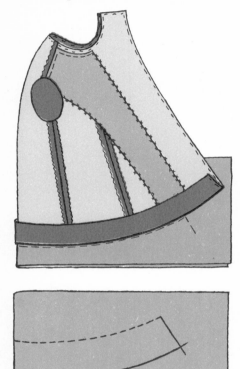

Finishing hems

Pin the lower edge of the interfacing along the fold edge of the hem on the inside. Catch-stitch this edge to underlining. Smooth interfacing into the rest of the coat. Pin and catch-stitch the upper edge to the underlining. On a princess-line coat, it is attached the same way. It is necessary to ease in the hem on this style of coat. Sew along the edge of the hem with a large machine stitch. Ease the fullness in on this thread so that the hem fits smoothly to the inside of the coat.

Sew a seam binding to the edge of the hem. Pin the hem to the inside of the coat and then catch-stitch the hem only to the interfacing.

The interfacing is sewed into a straight coat in the same way. Be sure to measure the fullness at the hem of the coat from the pattern. If the interfacing is too large, it will stretch the coat and the hem will ripple. A tight interfacing will cause it to pucker.

The straight hem can be pinked or finished with a seam binding, depending on the weight of the coat. Turn

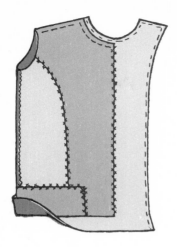

the hem and then catch-stitch it to

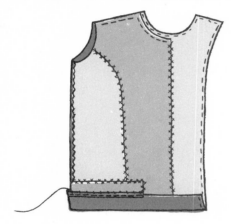

underarm seam; catch-stitch it down.

The top edge of the interfacing is catch-stitched to inside of sleeve.

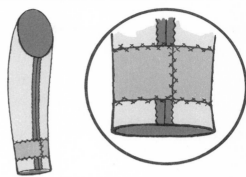

Turn up hem and catch-stitch to the interfacing.

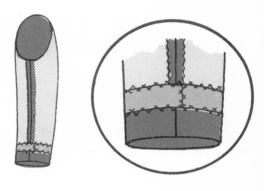

the interfacing. For a coat with a lapel, follow the pattern instructions on how to correctly roll the lapel and apply the collar and facings.

Sleeves

Turn the sleeve on the hem mark. If the sleeve will be let down later, the hem will be deeper than is generally allowed in coat sleeves. Press the hem back on the sleeve. Next cut a strip of interfacing on the bias, 2 inches wider than the hem.

Catch-stitch one edge along the fold edge of the hem and on the inside of the sleeve. Then lap the interfacing where it comes together at the

Setting in the sleeve

Sleeve will be easier to set if easing stitch is used at cap. Using a large stitch, sew from underarm around cap, back to underarm. Make 2 rows of stitching, one on seam allowance line, second $\frac{1}{4}$ inch in from sleeve edge. Ease fullness around sleeve. About 1 inch at top of sleeve is flat, with fullness eased in on either side. Pin sleeve underarm to coat underarm. Pin, matching front and back notches. Pin top of sleeve to shoulder seam. Ease sleeve fullness to fit armhole. Pin sleeve with pins on seam allowance line, parallel to seam. Start at underarm on sleeve side; sew sleeve in, removing pins as you go.

Lining a coat

A coat pattern always includes pieces for the lining. Make any alterations in the lining that you made in the coat. Cut the lining from the lining pattern. Mark and sew any darts or tucks in the lining. The back of the lining has a pleat for ease. Press it for the entire length. Sew by machine across the top close to the neck to hold the pleat in place.

Sew up the side seams and shoulders. Press open all the seams of the lining. Lap shoulder seam of lining over shoulder seam of coat. Tack the seams together. Lap the side seam of the lining over the side seam of the coat and pin to fit. Tack the seams together, to about 6 inches from the coat bottom. Clip to seam allowance line all around back facing. Turn under a 5/8-inch seam, lap to seam allowance at back facing and pin.

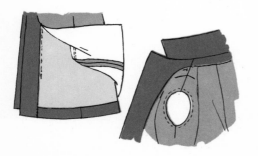

Turn under the seam allowance at front and lap it over front facing. Pin along both fronts. Sew lining in by hand. Hem lining, coat separately.

Sew up the sleeve lining. Place the wrong side of the sleeve lining against the wrong side of the sleeve. Tack the seams together by hand. Turn coat inside out so the coat sleeve is inside the lining sleeve. Turn under the seam allowance at the top of sleeve lining and lap it over the armhole seam allowance. Pin lining in place. Sew the sleeve lining by hand.

Turn under the lining at the lower edge of the sleeve, and pin over the edge of the hem. Slip-stitch by hand.

The hem of the lining should be made as deep as the hem on the coat so it can also be let down when the coat is lengthened. Also make the sleeve lining longer and turn up the extra length in the sleeve until it is ready to be lengthened.

Zip-in linings

A zip-in lining, which converts a spring coat to winter weight, is a practical way to get more wear. This lining can be made of wool plaids, checks, fleeces, fake furs, or any fabric that will add warmth to the coat.

You must plan for this lining before you begin to sew the coat, and use a slightly different construction. The lining used for spring weight remains in the coat. The extra-warm lining zips over this one.

When you make the coat with a lightweight lining, follow the same instructions just shown for lining a coat. There is one exception: At the front you usually lap the raw edge of the lining over the raw edge of the facing; instead, bring the raw edge of the lining under the facing and sew it firmly by hand to the underlining. Bind the raw edge of the facing with a piece of bias cut from the lightweight lining.

Now measure from the center back of the facing along this edge to about 2 inches from the finished length of the coat. If the length is 50 inches, buy two 24-inch-long separating zippers. Mark the center back of the coat facing. Lap the facing over one zipper, with the separating end of the zipper at the back of the facing, and the top of the zipper at the lower end of the facing toward the hem. The bound edge of the facing should lap to the center of the zipper chain. Sew the zipper in place along the right side of the facing, about $\frac{1}{2}$ inch in from the edge. Sew the second zipper in the same way, so that both zippers separate at back of neck.

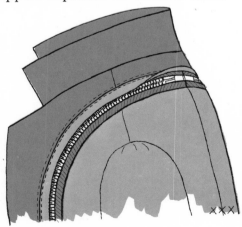

Cut the zip-in lining from the same pattern. Sew it together. Turn the hem 2 inches shorter than the coat. Trim away $1\frac{1}{4}$ inches of the front edge and bind this the same as the facing. Lap the lining over the top of the zippers sewed in the facing, so that the bound edges of the facing and lining meet. Sew the zipper in place from the lining side the same as on the facing. The heavy lining can be zipped in or out and the inside of the coat is always completely finished with a quality lining.

Sleeves

If the coat has a set-in sleeve, it is better to make the zip-in lining without sleeves, and just bind the armhole. If the coat has a raglan sleeve, the same sleeveless lining can be zipped in, or the sleeve edge of the heavy lining can be finished by applying knitted cuffs. These cuffs also act as windbreaks and add warmth.

Peter Pan collar

This collar is used most on children's coats. Often, it is made so that it is convertible to an open or notched collar. The coat pattern provides an upper and lower collar pattern. The under collar is cut on the bias with a center seam. Cut an interfacing of hair canvas from the same pattern. Sew and press this seam open on both under collar and hair canvas. Stitch back seam allowances on interfacing on both sides. Trim seams close to this stitching. Pin interfacing to wrong side of under collar, along the center seam. Roll the collar over your index finger. Start the padding stitch from center of the collar.

Work in a circle, but inside the seam allowance lines. Work back and forth in an ever-widening circle through center of collar. Fill in either side with a padding-stitch.

As you work, roll the collar over your finger, easing the collar as you sew. The edges of collar should curl back toward the center of the collar if it is rolled correctly.

Trim off the interfacing seam al-

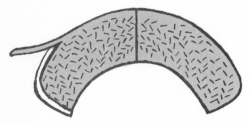

lowances all around. Pin the under collar to the upper collar, right sides together. Pin on the interfacing side. Sew all around the edge of the inter-

facing, easing in the upper collar a little as you pin and sew it in place. Then you can trim off the seam allowance to graduated widths.

Turn the collar right side out and baste all around, bringing the under collar in just slightly from edge.

Press the collar this way. Roll it over your hand with the right side of the collar up. Do a diagonal basting on the roll line.

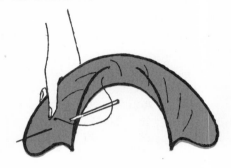

Put the collar face down on the table and roll the neck edges back, as you do for a dress collar, and pin the edges together all around the neck.

The upper collar edge may be a little short of the under collar edge, but if it rolls that way, then sew it the same way. The collar is made and the roll line sewed in before it is applied to the garment. This collar can be used on a cardigan-neck jacket.

Letting out a coat

It's always a good idea to buy some

extra fabric when you make children's clothes. The fabric can be used later for altering or for letting out garments as the child grows.

On the princess and box coats, hems of sleeves and coat can be lengthened as the child grows taller. This is usually the only alteration that is needed during the first year.

Later, the shoulders of the princess coat may have to be made larger. A straight box coat has an easy fit, so shoulders may not need adjusting.

You can increase shoulder size on the princess style by setting in a straight strip of fabric in the seam of the gores. This can also add a new decorative touch to the coat.

Remove the lining, since it must also be let out. Rip on the side gore in the back and the front.

No other changes will be necessary on the coat. Cut a strip of fabric the width the coat is to be increased, plus the seam allowances. Here are some decorative details that can be added when you alter coat.

View 2

On this coat, the strip was cut into three lengths, and faced to form small points. Then it was sewed together, buttons were sewed on the points, and then inserted into the coat. It adds a decorative trim, in addition to providing extra size for added wear.

View 1

This style shows a strip of fabric tucked across before it is sewed to the coat. It makes a pretty trimming.

View 3

This view shows a strip cut to flare at the bottom, then pressed to form pleats. The addition of this strip of fabric allows enough ease for considerable growth. A pocket flap can be sewed on to give more detail.

Boys' coats

The construction of a boy's coat is very similar to a girl's. For young tots, the only differences are in color, the type of fabric, and the fact that the boy's coat buttons left side over right. In an older boy's coat, there is a definite style difference, as well as fabric choice, but the basic sewing technique is the same.

One style difference is the frequent use of a raglan sleeve in boys' coats. This sleeve fits more easily over the heavier clothes a boy wears. Also, boys' coats are usually made of heavier fabrics, such as tweeds, so an underlining is seldom needed.

A raglan sleeve is much easier to make than a set-in sleeve. The sleeve usually forms a part of the shoulder as well. The top shoulder seam is sewed up, then joined to the front and back of the coat. Underarm seam is sewed last, joining underarm of sleeve and side of coat all at once.

The raglan type of sleeve can also be used on a girl's coat.

Boys pants

Patterns for boys' slacks give a waist and inseam size. Buy the pattern according to the correct size of the waist.

Measure a boy for the inseam and outside seam for the correct length. Compare inseam measurement to the one given on the pattern. If the pattern has to be made longer or shorter, check outside seam measure of the pattern before you make the alteration. On the front slack pattern piece, measure from waistline to the finished length on the outside seamline. If it must be lengthened or shortened the same amount as for the inseam, then make necessary adjustment across leg below crotch. Pattern indicates where you should make this alteration.

If the outside of the slack seam measures longer or shorter in proportion to inseam measurement, an adjustment must be made between waist and crotch to insure a proper

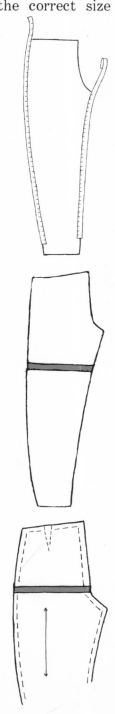

fit. Follow the pattern guide as you lay out the pattern for cutting. Mark the fabric carefully for darts, pockets, and other detail. Sew in the darts. Then press carefully.

Few boys' patterns show back pockets in the pants. If you want to duplicate a man's slacks more exactly, see instructions for making hip pockets, as well as other men's clothing, in the Creative Sewing Book on *Sewing Casual Clothes*.

It is easier to put the zipper in boys' pants while they are in the early stages of assembly and easier to handle. Join the center front seam to the mark indicated in the pattern. Use a skirt type zipper for fly front.

Your pattern will show two right fly facings and one left fly facing. If the fabric is lightweight, these can be cut from same fabric. If your slacks are of heavy fabric, face the right fly pieces with a lining fabric. Put the right sides of the two right fly pieces together, stitch them all around. Leave just top edge open. Turn right side out and press.

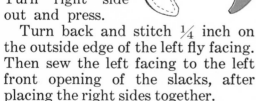

Turn back and stitch ¼ inch on the outside edge of the left fly facing. Then sew the left facing to the left front opening of the slacks, after placing the right sides together.

Clip and trim the seam and press

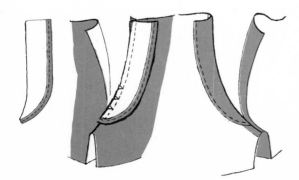

the seam carefully to inside of pants.

Place the zipper right side down at the right front opening, with the tape of the zipper along the seam edge. Sew as closely as possible to the teeth of the zipper with the zipper foot on your sewing machine.

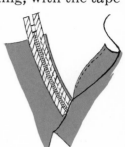

Turn the zipper right side up. The seam allowance is turned back. Slide your right facing piece under the zipper with about ½ inch extending beyond the zipper tape. (It will depend on the width of the right fly piece. It should extend under the zipper for width of the seam allowance.)

Stitch along the fold edge of the seam, close to the zipper. Catch fly piece in stitching as you sew.

Now, lap the left front to seam allowance line, and then pin or baste in place.

Turn the slacks to the wrong side. The tape of the zipper will now be against the left facing only. Pin the tape just to the facing. Sew the tape close to the zipper teeth, using the zipper foot. Then sew a second row of stitching on the edge of the zipper tape and turn the slacks to the right side. Fold the right fly extension back. Then mark and stitch on the outside of the slacks; be sure to catch back the left facing. Extension will now fall in place under the zipper. Reinforce the low-

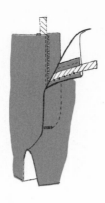

er end of the fly on the right side with a bar tack, catching all thicknesses of material with the tack. If the zipper is longer than the placket, unzip it and cut it off at the top when the waistband is sewed on to the slacks.

Side pockets

When a lightweight fabric is used for slacks, the same fabric can be used for the pockets. If you are using a heavier fabric, then make the pockets of a lightweight lining fabric, with facings used where they are sewed into the pants.

Cut a strip of the pants fabric about 2 inches wide. Turn under one edge $\frac{1}{4}$ inch and baste. Lap over each side of pocket piece and sew into place on the right side.

Pin the right side of pocket to the right side of front of pants, match-

ing notches. Stitch. Clip to medium dot. Trim the seam. Turn pocket to inside. Fold pocket so back pocket section is against front pocket section, right sides together. Stitch top fold of pocket piece to top of front pants. At base of pocket below the clip mark, stitch pocket to side of front pants.

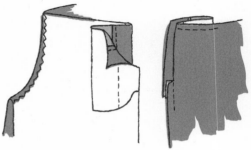

Turn to wrong side and stitch lower edge of the pocket only below clip mark. Put right side of the back and front pants pieces to-

gether and stitch along side seam. Be sure to stitch just inside line of stitching that holds pocket piece in

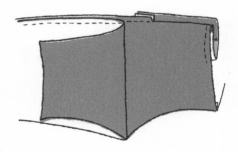

place. Next, join the pants together at the crotch seam.

Lining pants

Ski pants, leggings, and other pants made for cold weather are usually lined. Use a lining of wool or cotton flannel, or any other fabric that will add warmth.

Cut the lining from the same pattern as the pants, except make the legs 1½ inches shorter. Pants and lining are made up before the fly is made. Put wrong side of lining against wrong side of pants. Baste together at the hemline of each leg and at the top of the pants. If top of pants is finished with a hem, baste to the hemline at the waist. (In this case, lining should be cut off at this point.)

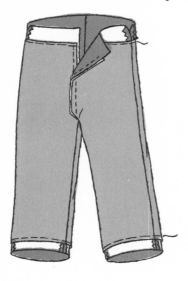

Finish the fly front as shown for unlined pants, page 59.

Pockets should be put in the pants before the lining is applied.

Turn under ¼ inch at the top of the pants and at the edge of each leg and stitch.

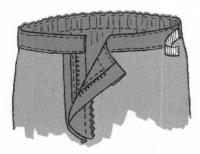

Turn down hem at waistline and then stitch in place by machine. Stitching will show on right side. Also stitch upper edge of pants, forming a casing. Rip a small opening in the side seams of the casing on the inside. Cut a piece of 1-inch elastic to an inch smaller than back waist measurement, and draw it through casing. Stitch into place at side seams of

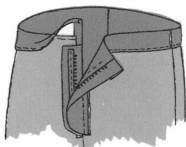

casing. Turn up lower edge of pants to form hem. Slip-stitch hem in place to lining. Unlined pants are turned up in same way, but must be carefully slip-stitched to inside of pants.

A waistband is sometimes used on boys' pants. Follow instructions on pattern for application.

If the trouser zipper is too long for the front opening of the pants, zip the head down and cut off the extra length of zipper at the waistline.

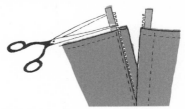

(Use trouser zipper for older boys' pants. It comes in an 11-inch length only, and is often too long for the fly length.)

Be sure to sew the waistband to the pants, catching tape of zipper in the waistline seam. This acts as the stop for the top of the zipper. The zipper head locks into place at any point when the tab is depressed.

INDEX